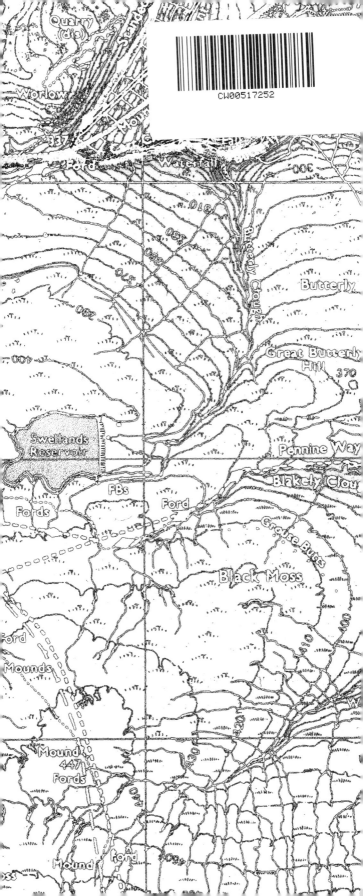

Simon Armitage New Cemetery

Norwich
UNESCO *City of Literature*

First published in 2017

by Propolis Books
The Book Hive
53 London Street
Norwich NR2 1HL

www.propolisbooks.co.uk

© Simon Armitage, 2017

Design & art by niki medlik at **studio medlikova**

A CIP record for this book
is available from the British Library

Printed and bound by PUSH, London, UK

Simon Armitage New Cemetery

propolis

To be continued.

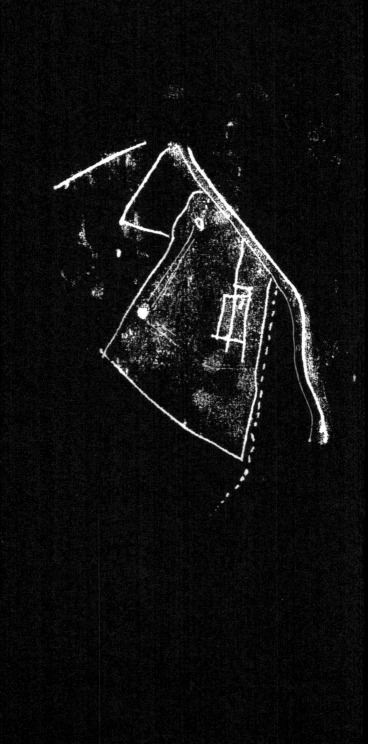

So the new cemetery
        goes ahead, bulldozers
                peeling back turf

from those level fields
        above Berry Brow, yellow diggers
                clawing at dark soil

in the pitched shadow
        of Castle Hill.
                Dear Kirklees Council, I say

plough all you like;
        better the deceased
                than others like me:

hippopotami of the shopping aisles,
        weed-killer gardeners,
                Haribo chefs

in combat pyjamas
        burning the midnight oil.
                Let tomorrow's estate

be a tended map of gravel paths,
        a yew tree roundabout,
                a single standpipe

and dripping tap, metal vases
        blown on their side, lines and lanes
                of headstones and graves

like nursery beds.
        Shore up the good earth
                with the green dead.

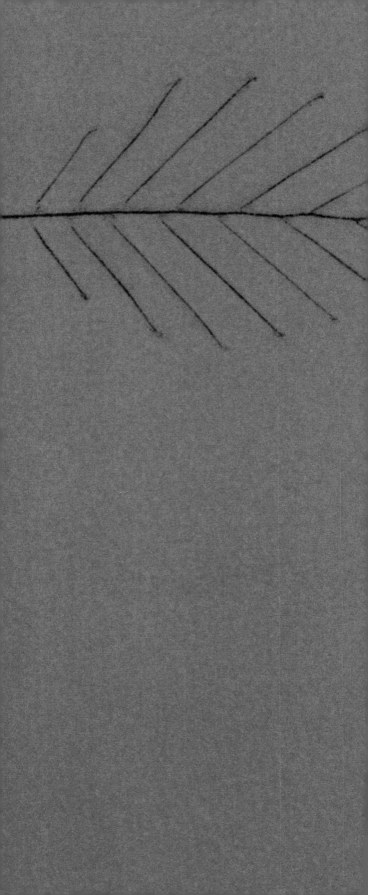

Reader, today
　　　　the poet has gone
　　　　　　　to his shed,

to the stripped-back world
　　　　of a wooden chair, an old desk.
　　　　　　　He has his themes:

dirty clouds over Farnley Tyas,
　　　　an irregular heart,
　　　　　　　dry beech leaves

veined with meaning.
　　　　Is it fair to say
　　　　　　　it is still morning?

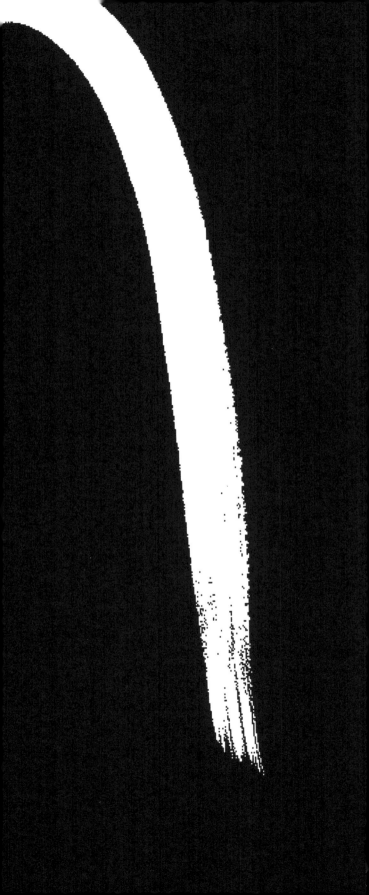

How much water
        can I cup in my palm,
                will pool in my hand?

Enough to wet the lips
        or splash the brow
                on the hottest day of the year

so far.
        He wouldn't budge
                when they built the dam,

stole back to the farm,
        went under
                with coal in his pockets

and fire in the hearth.
        A weathercock breaks the surface
                in seasons of drought.

A waterfall pours between
        finger and thumb,
                a torrent flows

through the gorge of the lifeline
        and over wrist.
                But an hour on,

what I lift to my face
        are crystals of salt,
                dead fish.

Dear planet,
      this morning the poet
         has gone

to his shed, back
      to the drawing board
         of four bare walls,

a small door,
      a single window pane.
         Today's simple task:

to answer the question
      every person alive
         always wanted to ask.

The tinsiest of red spiders
      touches down
         on the ruled ledger, occupies

open pages.
      Grey skies.
         Seven billion faces.

A cheap ballpoint
          usually does the trick,
                    just enough drag and flow,

like this one, striped
          with the faded name
                    of a Munich hotel.

Fine-grained snow
          like old-fashioned static
                    fell into the night, blanking

the tiled rooftops.
          At the writing desk
                    in an attic room

I pushed forward, except
          every fifteen minutes
                    a sensor detected

no movement,
          no signs of life, and turned out
                    the one light bulb.

Padlocks gripping
a public footbridge
over the Seine,

The kitchen window
        distraught with steam,
                my mother at the twin-tub

manhandling shirts,
        hauling drowning sailors
                from ocean to deck.

Reader, allow
            the poet to elegise
                        the ash:

that bank of saplings
            on Farnley Estate,
                        rankled with blight

after two seasons;
            this felled centenarian
                        culled with an axe:

on a muted TV
            some Danish backwoodsman
                        opens the bark,

reaches in
            through the flaked timber
                        and breaded grain,

scoops out
            its pulped heart
                        with his pink hand.

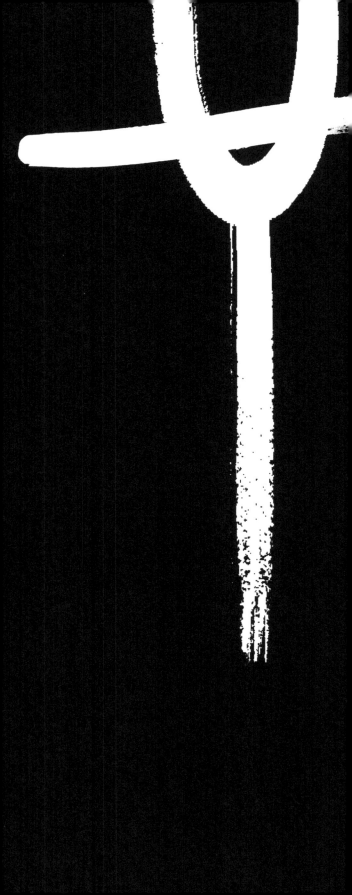

On the raw shoulder
      of Royd Edge, the upper limb
            of a storm-snapped beech

has ended up wedged
      on a lower branch.
            A little finger

will easily rock
      that two-pronged bough
            in the tree's crook,

but no amount
      of deranged swinging
            can begin to unhook

the dead from the living.
      The winds of the world
            blast and rattle

that private wood,
      and the wishbone rides
            in the tuning fork.

Metallic black 4x4s,
        sixty grand each,
                a cortège of five

slewing and churning
        hill to field
                and field to copse,

hounding a fox.
        And the same five
                later that day

parked nose to tail
        on Market Street,
                muddied bodywork

bearing the stripe
        of coin or door-key
                ploughed across paint.

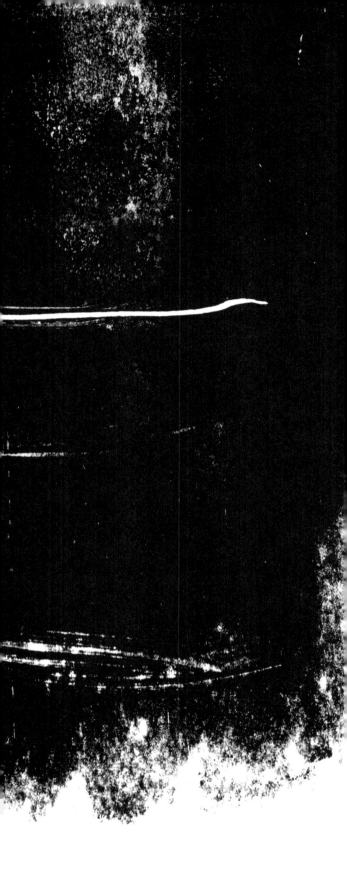

I wouldn't call it *my scene*,
        but I like the trumpeter's brown suede shoes,
           the pianist's Crimplene shirt,

the boozed-up uncle
        of the double bass,
           unsteady, wurring his slurds.

Sitting cross-legged,
        the percussionist rolls out
           his picnic blanket of odds and ends:

a Tibetan singing bowl,
        a jingle stick, a rattlesnake tail,
           a shaky egg,

a plastic shampoo bottle
        loaded with beads.
           I take my seat

next to a fellow poet
        whose twin brother
           died last month *in his sleep*.

Dear November,
      your open-fingered
            horse-chestnut leaves,

your leprous handshakes,
      your lost gloves on the wet path,
            do they offer or ask?

Today the poet
        repairs his shed,
                last night's storm

having scalped from the roof
        some forty square feet
                of weatherproof felt,

lifting and slinging the job lot
        into next door's field.
                The new felt tightly rolled

and stiff with frost,
        the bitumen stubborn,
                reluctant, a coma

of ink-black oil
        in a tin pot, my fingertips numb
                to the swarm of clout nails

in the canvas bag.
        But I haul up to a smooth platform
                of raw wood,

to a dozen strips
        of unseasoned pine
                taking the winter sun.

I'll sprawl here a while,
        a sky-diver held
                two yards from the ground,

all heaven above, a desk and chair
        underneath, the shirt
                on my back already fouled

with the labour and toil
        of a hard week's thinking
                and half a poem.

Four in the morning,
            three days running,
                        asleep then awake,

disturbed by the voice
            of a railway worker's
                        recorded announcement, hailed

to the unmanned station,
            hailed
                        from a square-mouthed speaker

high on a stanchion,
            making it known
                        to the empty platform

that the last train out of Deadville
            is cancelled.
                        Repeat cancelled.

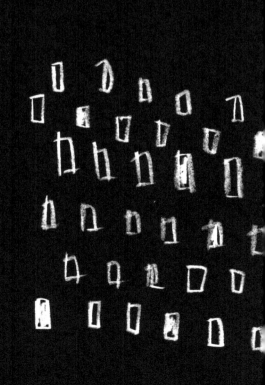

The new cemetery's shaping up.
        A stone-built lych-gate
                doubles as bin-store and toilet block.

The departed are yet to arrive
        so the numbered plots lie undisturbed,
                but the roads are laid out:

avenues of virgin tarmac
        leading to turning-circles and cul-de-sacs,
                and there's no barrier,

so day and night the site crawls
        with dog walkers, adulterers
                and learner drivers.

They forced the door
        and found in the bed-sit
                the pulsing hook-line

of diamond on vinyl,
        the arm still ploughing
                the run-out spiral,

the lost module
        of cartridge and stylus
                in captured orbit

around the spindle, a looped,
        circling, whirl-pooling swansong
                that died as they craned up

the weightless needle
        and lowered him down
                on the rope that he swung from.

Dear reader,
        this evening the poet
                has gone to his shed,

to temper his thoughts
        in the prayer-shaped furnace
                of a candle's flame,

to throw with his hand
        wild shadow-puppets
                onto the starched page. So what

if there's nothing to say:
        this poem, born of itself,
                for its own sake.

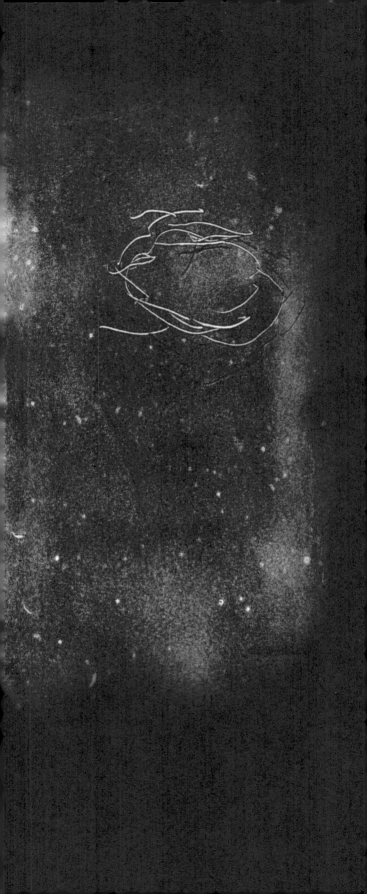

The years build nests
        out of old hair.
                How they

orbit the sun
        but return
                to the same belfries and spires

bewilders
        even the best minds.
                No storm at sea

can deplete them.
        And bare
                gullible trees,

like children of famine,
        reach upward
                to meet them.

Dear universe,
I shaved this morning –
look at these

fine black pinpricks
constellated
in the white sink.

The new moon
of this nail clipping
proves I'm alive,

and once every couple of months
I re-grow a fringe.
Universe, it's against you

I measure myself:
the laws of thermodynamics
are calling my warm atoms

into deep space,
but for now
I'm holding

this hair, these bristles,
this middle finger
up to your dumb face.

Can a berth be reserved?
This western sector
not *christened* yet,

ground unbroken, turf intact.
Laced with preservatives
wooden telegraph poles

embalm the day,
hoist live power-lines
fizzing in damp air

above hawthorn and dwarf birch.
A spooked blackbird
trapezes low

over a mown verge.
Here a body lies
angled, inclined towards

semaphoring turbine blades
on Scapegoat Hill
or the silhouette shack

of the shooting lodge
under Scout Rock.
Here the skull is aligned,

eye-sockets fired
by moor-blaze
necklacing nabs and crowns,

or low red sun
igniting the fonts
of Butterley, Blakeley,

Swellands, Cupwith,
Redbrook, Sparth, Wessenden,
Wessenden Head,

Deer Hill, March Haig,
Tunnel End, Black Moss
and Little Black Moss.

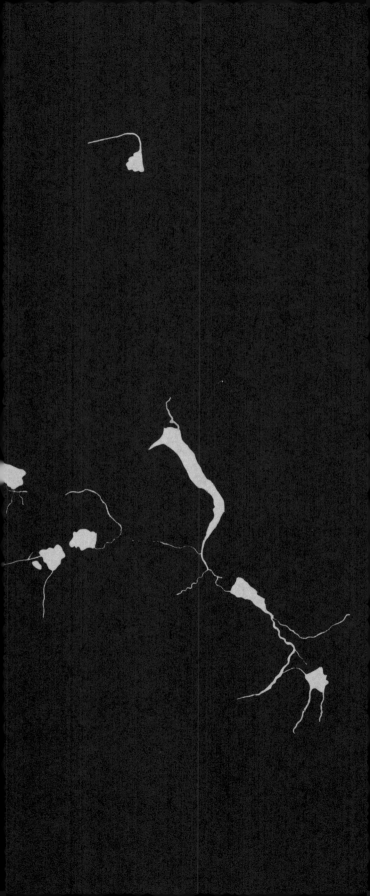

Acknowledgements are due to Plume magazine and smith|doorstop books.

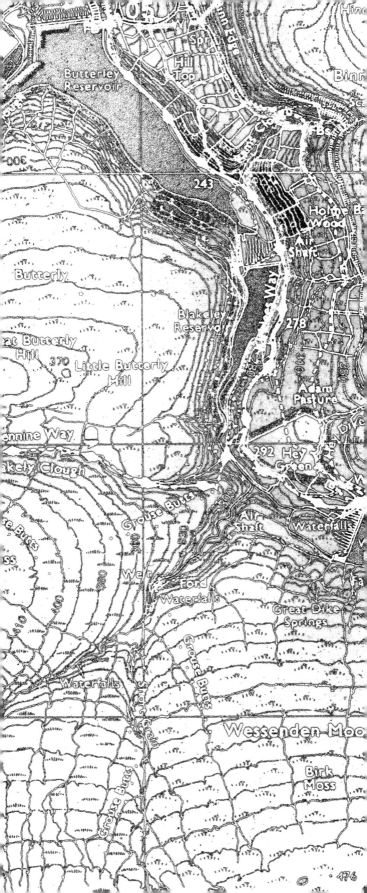